CSU Poetry Series IX

Jeanne Murray Walker

NAILING UP
THE HOME SWEET HOME

Cleveland State University Poetry Center

ACKNOWLEDGMENTS

Grateful acknowledgment is made to the publications in which the following poems have appeared.

"A Bestiary For the Birth of Christ," in JAWBONE
"After the Suicide," in ASPEN ANTHOLOGY
"All that Flashes," in KTAADN
"Answer to a Lover" (formerly "Answer to a Poet Lover"), in CRITICAL QUARTERLY
"Ariadne," in POETRY
"Building Home," in DESCANT (Toronto)
"Cartoon for Shostakovich's First Symphony," in THE CHRISTIAN SCIENCE MONITOR
"Complaint: To William Carlos Williams," in BALL STATE UNIVERSITY FORUM
"Deliver Me, O Lord, from My Daily Bread," in CIMARRON REVIEW
"Driving North to the Headwater" first appeared in THE CHARITON REVIEW, vol. 5, no. 2 (Fall, 1979)
"Haydn's Creation: Ardmore Presbyterian Church, 1978," in KENYON REVIEW
"How Things Happen," in AMERICAN POETRY REVIEW
"How This World Needs Keys," copyright 1977 by Washington and Lee University, reprinted from SHENANDOAH: the Washington and Lee Review, with the permission of the editor
"Illness in the Afternoon," in COUNTRY OF THE RISEN KING
"Knowledge of Trees," in MASSACHUSETTS REVIEW
"On the Language Which Writes the Lecturer," in THE AMERICAN SCHOLAR
"Prometheus," in MILKWEED CHRONICLE
"Pythagoras Understands His Theorem," in MILKWEED CHRONICLE
"She Brings Him Home," in DESCANT (Toronto)
"The Blackhaired Carpenter," in THE NEW ENGLAND REVIEW
"The Proposition of Ourselves," in ASPEN ANTHOLOGY
"The Statue in Spring," in NANTUCKET REVIEW
"Their Wedding," in WASCANA REVIEW
"There Conveys Meaning," in POETRY
"Useful Work," in POETRY NOW
"What the West Wind Knows," in ST. ANDREW'S REVIEW

The CSU Poetry Center expresses its gratitude to the Ohio Arts Council for a grant which aided the publication of this book.

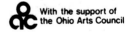

With the support of
the Ohio Arts Council

Distributed by NACSCORP, Inc., Oberlin, Ohio, and by FIELD, Oberlin College, Oberlin, Ohio

CONTENTS

III.

For Mother

I.

ALL THAT FLASHES

I watched my grandfather
take another fish out of the tub.
Eyes blank as thumbtacks,
she beat her tail against the block,
her coral gills laboring up and down.
He ripped the sequined skin from her back.

You hurt her, I accused.
Yaii, the old man laughed.
One of these days I'll ask her.

But I know when I have seen a fish suffer.
And when I think of that,
nothing bright is free from pain:
the eyes of young girls reading books,
eternity, enraged by clocks,
a lover's flashing hands,
the neon fires beneath the skin of rocks.

HOW THINGS HAPPEN

In Lincoln, Nebraska the bell rings
and a woman leans across a desk in classroom 243,
tugging at her white banlon sweater
while she lists the governors from Ashton C. Shallenberger on down.
Hearing a truck outside fail, strip and grind uphill,
her voice skids on a name and goes down.
A fly sizzles and lights on the spiral of a notebook
over which a child bends to erase the name.

Two miles down the street, past houses
you would say were all in the same monotone,
a man in a stone ranch-house leans against the sink,
listening to the regular boom of blood in his wrists.
He is stitching a gauze herb-bag for vegetable soup,
peas, tomatoes, beans, the minimum a child needs to live,
when he thinks he hears on the straightaway outside
a truck catch and growl uphill,
making him forget to listen for the boom.

It is time for the bell to ring.
The bell rings and the child
lets the governors fall to the balls of her feet.
Imagine her walking past carnations deadly
as the gills of slain fish. Past birchtrees
thrust into brown lawns like war staves.
She walks until red moths bang on her eyelids.

When she turns the corner of 54th Street
in the driveway beside the coupe
three men from an emergency squad are at work.

Years later, she finds the soup.

STORY PROBLEM: DIRECTIONS FOR THE CAMERA

Focus on LeVila Simmons, hiking up
her gathered, red plaid skirt above the knee
in ninth grade math. Through the air
paper planes did figure-eights and on
the board Gunwale Gordon neatly wrote
tomorrow's problems, keeping his cool blue eye—

cocking the trigger of his dangerous eye—
at the absolute zero of LeVila's knee. Up
the row Irving got out his pen and wrote
on virgin oak GORDON SUCKS VILE'S KNEE.
Then he slumped down, laying his head on
his desk and glowering into the stagnant air

of a stagnant world where older men fall heir
to every pretty girl in turn, while I,
behind him, shuddered. What would a wife put on
or take off in their crackerbox house, just up
the road where he lived, to erase that knee
from his mind? His wife's skin must have seemed rote,

even to herself, as the graph paper I wrote
his answers on, since everything, even the air
around his hands, and finally LeVila's knee,
grew humdrum in his calibrated eye.
LeVila flunked. The rest of us moved up
from plain figures to geometry and on,

getting prettier as we went. But focus on
LeVila, now in a purple dress, who wrote
sums all the next year, who tallied up
the figures over and over, only to err
and err again. Focus on her eye
as it films over, move to her sweet, pink knee

to the mole on her lip, grown darker, to an eye
that's fixed. Move up. Then through the air
to the lost knee, the final problem that he wrote.

USEFUL WORK

Standing in sunlight which sheared
off his left arm
my father
flicked dust from our bronze Packard
and ordered
me off the running board.
He was wearing his shirt
with blue peacocks walking in it
and he held the keys.
I refused to go, staring
a peacock in its red fabric eye
for as long as it took my father's swat
to dish me into the garden.

The beans there hid themselves
beneath heart-shaped leaves and
grew an inch an hour.

He leveled a look down
the beanrow
straight as his seeding eye
had seen that Spring
and slammed the car door shut.

Turning the key in the ignition,
he backed across the gravel
by the tiger lilies
and drove off
straight to death.

A long time now
I have been waiting
for wheels in the driveway

my fingers crashing among
the vines
delivering the beans
into this battered aluminum pan.

PUTTING THINGS IN PLACE

I root for a man the size of a thimble
who snags a fly, pegs the ball to first, licks
his thumbs and yanks his pants up
dizzy years away, down on the field.

In the pulse of twilight the tiny man
dwindles and throbs like the vibrato of the organ
sobbing take me out to the ball game.
This inning nobody got home.

Grandfather, I am thinking how you learned to strand
men on base playing shortstop for the Yankton farm team
while hitched horses steamed
in sun, patient as loaves of bread,
and my mother, the dark child, dawdled beneath a hoof.

You've trapped me on this base needing to go beyond
what you rehearsed before you died, your hand
flying to your veined temple like a bullet every time,
how you zinged out of Illinois by stolen train
and earned five farms with two good hands.
I don't know how, or what they looked like.
I can't remember who you sold them to, or if you sold them
whether you got rooked or thought you did.

My memory has grazed north, along deep runs
of Minnesota fences with no guess
which grass belonged to you, where your barbed wire
stretched its wounded back to keep your cattle in.

You were always on the other side.

But I would rather stand on base forever with a three-two count
or in your basement when I was thirteen, flooded
with the bright stink of horseradish
you ground until our eyes streamed tears
and our lungs flopped hopeless in the air
than to have stood once beside you, stopped

in your final box
struck out of every game I know,
your smart hands still, your farms gone out of you.

Maybe for all the organ's brag
none of us gets home
and yet I keep trying to find a way we all win once,
imagining that even though the last horse may be dead or sold,
the fields leased out to ragweed
the time will come, you will tag up and steal home safe
because I will have stepped back and called a catch
straight into the pocket of my waiting glove.

FALLING HEIR

Parkers Prairie, Minnesota. There
the grain elevator thumped its chest
on the edge of town; one stoplight shut its eye
all night and Murray was a good enough name
to get you into Susan Schamber's parties,
where girls refused to slumber. While the air
was bruised by sunset, on the bed you threw

yourselves down with yearbooks, paging through
until you found a sixteen-year-old there
whose pretty mouth grew gaudy in the air
of twilight and you could dream the rest: her chest
no longer covered by boy's undershirts, the eye
that trumps a fullback's eye in class, and parties
at Lilac Lake every weekend. Her name,

whatever the letters said, was always your name.
You dreamed of being sixteen and lilac through
and through, of tempting Hallins—the parties
on your party line—to slander beyond their
gifts, which were not great. But father's eye
and spanking hand, which could astonish air,
kept you at plain eight. Your own chest,

stalling behind your dream, remained the chest
of an ordinary child whose ordinary name
could get her to birthday parties, through the air
of a Spring day, home from school, then through
a piano lesson. The records are straight; the eye
in the school photo is clear. What parties
began at Schamber's also ended there.

But dreams of your name also began there.
Plain as the flannel poultice on your chest
you wore at eight when you had croup—to parties
and to bed—no matter—plain as the name
you bore, was an inheritance your eye
could never see but which ignited air
like your mother's lilac scent as she blazed through

your bedroom late at night. You learned it through
lilac: through all things there by not being there.
In that bedroom, once struck sick, you choked on air
and listened to the rattle in your chest.
Plain things must rise above themselves. Not your eye
but some angle of vision turned everything to parties
and parties, at last, became your real name—

your inheritance, a dream: your mother's name was there.
Rising to life through failing eye and chest,
you learned your name at last by falling heir.

ONE LAST GAME

Stamping through the cold air
blowing on our fingernails in the schoolyard
where grass whiskered the cement even when we were children
we gather for one last game.
The minutes of the rest of our lives
now already empty of one another's presences
rumble past like boxcars
over the crossing
on their long way to our graves.

Above us our steep fathers bear high snows,
their granite riddled with faults of love
still visible from our childhoods.

But there is not time in this breathless schoolyard
to ponder the bulk of their deaths
for our shadows are driven like sheep
to and fro by the shadow of the fox.
Before we can fashion a prisoners' base,
before we can agree on rules for calling Time,
they are driven
between the goal-lines of vows
drawn by our eager hands long ago
and a voice snagged by something like joy cries
Run Sheep Run.

FARM GARDEN IN MINNESOTA

Hot wind stings grit down planted rows
of nothing yet, just sprouting. With luck
in three months it may swim in Mason jars.
But North will take what it can first.
They say it's beat the odds to drive hail down
three years running, smashing crops to stubble.
North still holds hail in its mouth to spit
behind the geese it sends out every fall.

When they want to tell how hail bullies
and bullies until everything gives way, it's this:
Think of the day Henrietta wiped her hands
on a flour sack and took the news:
no oats, corn two thirds gone, not one
cucumber thick as a wrist to float in tubs
that summer. Hail changes everything.
She thinks of the five kids,
two tying on their shoes with twine already.
Smoothing the oilcloth, she says, we'll do.
She works the math on an envelope. He frowns,
but she says no. Egg money. I can make do
another year. This is the crop he came to gather.

After the screen door bangs shut behind him,
she steps out into this garden, where the hail
forgot to touch a peony bush. She snaps a flower off.
In her hands, it doesn't fall to tatters.

AFTER THE SUICIDE

Let's get this straight,
from the beginning we loved you.
Or as a substitute, we needed you
shaking your blond curls at us
like a spoiled god.
Your body mapped out the territory
we were lost from.
The quick blue eye,
your swagger, which broke into an easy lope,
the pout, lips the color of bricks.
Your hands were wild as cowlicks,
stars lodged beneath your fingernails.
A vein knocked in your temple
while you tried to teach us
how to tie knots tight as an apple
but we wanted fingers quick as yours.
Now on this warm May night
we imagine the scuttling of your shoes
on your coffin,
your body lying in state.
So it belongs to us at last.
Too late, we try to think.
What perfection did you imagine
that we could never see?
You, who broke
the promises of your veins
to us, it is possible we love you now.

ONE ANOTHER'S KIN: LONDON, AUGUST 1977

He found us, cutting through back alleys
in Belgravia at ten o'clock, when the sun
hewed out great blocks of light. Running
with luck by the bright doors for the sheer ease
of it, for the speed of having slept and eaten,
of having seen the Tower, Madame Tussaud's,
Harrod's, all of that done, and now on this last day
to be free and lit with sun! There in Belgravia
even the alleys were fine: mailslots, numbers,
brass doorknockers, every brick tuckpointed,
the trim painted cordial colors, tan or black.
He found us under a window box of geraniums.

His penny loafers lapsed to holes all over,
wearing a baggy tweed, he leaned and droned
in an Oxford accent of wife trouble, trouble
providing, the story of all our lives,
how he had been sick, a case of flu
lasting fourteen years. He stood beneath
the geraniums for twenty minutes slurring
the story before we guessed he wanted anything
or what he wanted. He wanted us to buy a song.
Fumbling, he coughed, and brushed away the snakes
from his doughface. His voice gone Irish,
his wheezy organ-grinder lungs piped out

the merchandise till we were no more tourists
but kin in the northern land he lived in,
cousined by a lullaby we knew but had forgotten,
the song all parents sing, all children know.
We paid the drunk from Oxford five pounds,
not knowing what it cost him. He took our notes
and we took his, though money buys neither song nor memory.
No wonder the bargain failed, that I sit now
trying to recall my father, or that tune,
hoping that down some street in London
one dying man still lugs my childhood
in the bushelbasket of his ribs.

ILLNESS IN THE AFTERNOON

Already ring on ring
and wheels in wheels
spinning our amber halo heavenward;
it's work, this turning.

And I, riding the calliope of a bright fever.
see things, for once, as they really are.
All of us here, as at table
for Christmas dinner,
with joy, with joy.
You, tender-eyed on a unicorn,
handing me a drink of water.
All of us riding swans, foxes, antelopes,
as we always will be, even
in our perishing to heaven.

I shudder, stretch,
scattering rings of brilliant pain.

COMPLAINT: TO WILLIAM CARLOS WILLIAMS

Caught on white space, here you lie
in a's and b's and c's, a sly
procession of ants marching by
to sting brains which, anyway, will die.

You never got a burial.
Your lurid flesh is never done.
No lowering to the tactful ground
but years of rotting in the sun.

For in your book the world is full,
muscular. And therefore kind.
The pages swarm. They glut and smell.
They are no white space of the mind.

You bloom a peach, at will, to flesh.
You raise a doorway and a leaf.
You cheek an old man's skull. You fill
the heart with raving bird and bell.

It is not true. It is not true,
for time's a thief. I have an eye.
Time took my father. Every clue.
Poet, on the page, you lie.

DRIVING NORTH TO THE HEADWATER

All day, the radio blares news
of twelve people who lost their lives on a showboat
overturned by a tornado in Ames, Iowa
while I start north to find you, my dark
headwater, my father. After twenty dry years
would you ask how it was? Would you be waiting
at the end as you must have waited
at the beginning? I will tell you.
Not to remember why I started
was the most blank forgetting of all.
While the white lane markers
sutured Delaware to New Jersey, New Jersey
to New York, I watched for signs
and grew thirsty. The highway played its hand
of green aces from Philadelphia
one after another, to Saratoga Springs.
Coming into Schenectady, I drove
through a wide band of country music
which somewhere further north began to fade,
the voices growing invisible as ghosts.
Rusty harvesters stood beside barns
which collapsed into waiting fields.
How was it? I will tell you.
I travelled all day without stopping,
without food, without water
for fear the car would not start again.
I kept my distance from the Kozy Kamper
full of children I could see
for a hundred miles in the rear view mirror,
its tire promptly buttoned onto its bumper.
Beside me trucks snarled up the mountains
corseted with rock, while I looked for you.
You did not come. I looked for you.
The roads grew narrower
until I turned down a lane beside an old lake
with reeds whiskering the shore,

trees up to their knuckles in sweet water.
When the needle on the gas gauge
registered EMPTY I thought:
Now come. Or don't come.
I am driving down the final lane and
daylight is shutting down. The only sign
reads NIGHTCRAWLERS FOR SALE. Finally I can see
nothing but the muscles of my arms, stiff
on the steering wheel, curving like yours
used to curve. Ahead I can feel
the bridge falling
asleep over the river, the fields
pulling up their covers to the road.
I can hear the lock lock lock
of the wipers which my hand has turned on,
the clouds finally having begun to give rain.

PRAYING FOR FATHER ON ALL SAINTS' DAY

Your smile still stirs apples, Papa. Molecules
of my dreams move when you turn over in
your death. Against rain the oak trees' muscles
tighten and endure, Old Patience, and the
pebbles, wearing your look, call me through streets.

How many days have I wandered
down this lane of laundromats and shops where
my sister is buying old crosses each noon,
past the tenements of soup in bright orange
kitchens at twilight where you evade me?

In the window of the bank I saw you
compose your smile. Before I could break the
glass your mouth blurred into the image on
a coin. I bought a handful to drop like
Gretel did on her way to the oven.

Today I will lie in some alley and throw
the tunes of Sunday songs over me like
dust. I want to be a beggar while you
stroll by, winking, tossing me one of your
buttons. I want your last wish to lie still

in my hand. I want my fingers, like the wings
of birds, to knock on the air and be let in.
I want to peel your shadow from ground. I
want to free you from the counterfeit of
stones, vegetables, faces. If the river

that flows by the 5 & 10 repeats your
name as often as my mother did, Old
Man, the noise will wear out new boots, make water
deaf. But you are dead. I come to the
church whose incense burns all day at your

altar. There broken doves dip in rafters while
the shuttle of light weaves the seasons. Hear?
The sound of nineteen years passing on the
shoulders of the heavy loom. Angels bear
this church away like dreaming figureheads

of a dark ship. But I am done with you,
my dodge, my fleet dead. I have come to give
you up, my strong ghost, my sweet parent long
since pushed into the ground as into an
oven. Now I want to blaze you from the earth.

With lilies and bells you go, the bright way
of all the loveliest things. Burn. Burn. The
fire rubs its legs like crickets. Burn until
not a button is left, not the sound
of a boot stamping in autumn air. Then

the oaks relax in avenues of sun.
The shuttle stops running its tedious
way. My feet quit pacing on their pavement
and at last you can meet my gaze with no
particular face, which is the final face,

gone to ashes and prayers. Your altar
breaks into song because the octaves
of trees can ring in it now, Father, Father,
Father, and I come home in this open
church, these clean streets, to your nimble cross.

II.

FINISHING THE HOUSE

Morning. I clench six nails
between my teeth and knock
a seventh home to seam
a bedroom floor, to lock
oak to plywood to beam.
This is my own hammer
but each blow falls
behind yours like a stammer.

I think back to the year
I learned to hold a pliers
and steady a leaping saw.
Before scrap-wood fires
until my hands were raw
I hacked at 2 x 4's
while you raised studs, drank beer,
and leveled oak floors.

At dusk you would cut off
the whinnying Black and Decker,
and after all the violent
banging of your hammer
we stood together, silent,
dreaming houses. Then
I thought your laugh
could finish what you'd begun.

Once as I grew up
when we drove home to mother,
she grabbed your blue plaid shirt
somewhere below your shoulder
to beat out the day's dirt.
You rocked back on your heels
while plaster dust flew up
like seven startled angels.

Now I run down the list,
frowning as you frowned
over saw, chisel, pail,
but remembering no sound
that winter, when your frail
heart's hammer tripped, and fell,
stiffening your fist
so you couldn't pound a nail.

The wind made paper waltz
through walls you hadn't done.
Packing up your hammer
we sold what you'd begun.
Finishing, now, I hear,
dust rising by my ear.
Angels in blue plaid shirts
rouse and climb the stair.

BUILDING HOME

My job is to pound this nail into the wall
and while you are gone I will
get it into the wall somehow.
I can use a pipewrench, my slipper, a beer can,
anything, just as long as the nail doesn't
turn into a dragon and fly away.
Since you say there is a nail
I assume there is a wall.
    Beside the wall stands the commode.
    Over there the steps rise to our bedroom.
    This is the blue chair where
    you sometimes sit and watch me while
    our window dices sunlight onto that rug.
    In the corner the cat yawns.
I will get this nail into the wall before you return.
I know there is a nail because
you are out catching dragons.
And I can pound a nail with almost anything.
Look at how I have built a home for us out of this poem.

DELIVER ME, O LORD, FROM MY DAILY BREAD

When paper bags wallow like demons
over the floor in orange dream kitchens
and a legion of groceries nods and winks
on the unrepentant cupboards,
deliver me, then, O Lord, to stones.
Let me not see jam grinning on the face
of whole wheat. Keep cake from rising
on my tongue like morning. May I
despise pizza and beer.
While lemon rings its high bells
and I kneel helpless
in the dark church of chocolate,
Father of slender angels and of the slightly fed,
Deliver me once more from my daily bread.

TURNING

The green tongues of the fern have disappeared
and rancor of broken apples fills the air.
The field tilts from the sun. My footprints take
a steep winter altitude. At four
o'clock the pond is locked with ice, a leaf
stuck on a stick. Beside the frozen hedgerow
foxes curl while trees burn blank. Human,
I cannot tell how dreaming slugs go stiff
but earth and I put on such terrible cold
that I turn back to your door. Inside I find
the bread, the wine, the silver crossed before
our plates. I know it all—your bookshelf, the deep
shadows between books. You grin and pile
more wood in the strong hands of the fire.

THE PROPOSITION OF OURSELVES

Yesterday I was as remote from you, from
the thought of you and me eating breakfast in this room
as the furthest, impeccable star is from my thumbnail.

Then we were the very proposition of ourselves,
as a chair is when it hesitates by the corner,
the rushes of its seat whiskering in blue shadow.

So many times I have walked into and out of the room
where the chair attends in silence that I no longer
have to notice how its design perplexes the shadow.

The chair has resolved itself into the corner
as the corner has resolved itself into the room,
which has no violence to change or to call to me.

How can it be that one day a chair speaks?
Light calls to the red wood of its patient back
and suddenly it appears, no longer obliged by shadow

no longer alien. It is a cousin. It is a lover.
Everything within me becomes a space which it might fill.
Everything about the chair grows visible and dear.

There is a cry that seems to arise from objects.
It is this desire I hear, arising from you now,
unanswerable as the cry arising from a chair
whose arms are finished, locked and permanent.

IN THE ECONOMY OF TREES

In the economy of trees, all has gone leafless
and together we make a sound inarticulate
as two sticks scraped on one another's thighs.
Where are you? Move over. Yes. There. There.
What follows could be the grammar of lost causes:
the lock picked, the cat run off, the silverware in hock,
the furniture untucked and gutted, rolled up rugs
and ashes strewn from room to room,
the final silence of a hearth which will not yield fire,
nothing to cook, no fire to cook with. Nothing.
Or this could be some phase, one dark, a ruin
which only threatens in the breach between summer
and summer. The trees will torch with green again
and catch their voices. Roses will ring on our trellises,
the sacked house turn out to be a dream gone.
These dry sticks are portents. We scan each tree
to predict what may become of this sky,
this poor house in the economy of you and me.

PRETEND THEY TAKE A WALK

Pretend that what the pines shed
lies on the ground like hundreds of compass needles
pointing all directions
and brown oak leaves strew
the sidewalk like
the hands of dead babies.

Say she takes it into her head
that the dead babies are hers,
that her future children
are falling down around her ears.

So she does the logical thing:
Grasping the nearest brass doornob,
she steps in,
locks the door,
throws the bolt like
a promise to die before her children do,
and begins to try
to keep her promise.

He stands outside the door
and reasons with her.
"We will have a baby live as a peony,"
he tells her.
Then he lays his ear against the door.

Inside, he hears her
trying to put the leaves back on the trees.

Reason having failed,
he inserts a file in the crack
and slices at the bolt.

He cannot get it; she is keeping her promise.

He hacks and pounds.
Then he stops to listen.

He can hear her arranging her hands
on the oak floorboards for the last time.

Pretend fall continues.

KNOWLEDGE OF TREES

The two of them stepping across the street
in spring, held down to earth by sunlight,
her arm around his back,
his hand across her shoulder while she thinks
how easy magnolias have it, merely to follow
their branches out of themselves
and into the air in thunderclaps of pink.
No search involved.
No rampaging back for the reverend grandparent
seed that set the hot pink off inside their hearts.
No nonsense about hearts.
No scrutiny of rings.
The trees go out of their heads without a fact to go on.
The two of them step up the curb at the corner
beside the trees with grey, factual bark,
and tilting their heads together in laughter now
they follow themselves beyond their footprints
down the sidewalk as if in time-lapse film.
She throws her foot into the vacant air
to walk and, falling forward, feels herself grow lighter
while traffic stops for hours
and her feet escape the final webs of sunlight.
All the blurred trees are waving goodbye to her now,
the magnolias, the elms, the oaks, the trees of grammar,
and her family tree.
The last thing she sees is her Aunt Evie's tyrannical eyebrow
signaling goodbye while she, who is free
with her knowledge of trees
to stay in this spring
decides to go
the way Aunt Evie's settee went out of itself
blossoming for months from its coils, noiselessly.

HOW THIS WORLD NEEDS KEYS

I stand outside the door to my office,
having just locked myself out, my keys in,
and think like a thief: how solid the door,
how solid myself, how this world needs keys.

Inside, the phone is not ringing. But inside
my head someone I desire decides
to call, to connect us with his hand.
His need worries facts. Who will answer?

Within, the keys stay themselves on the desk.
The books work inside their covers, going on
as usual with their harlots, plots, tulips.
In that other room in my head, the hand

lifts the receiver. He begins to dial.
The window, its plants, and their shadows
around the phone become a fiction of
themselves which cleave the air only in my mind.

Waste paper lies candid in an idea
basket and the very pencils inside
my office are not. Without a key all
grows holy and conceivable as wish.

Like the fond tongues of late afternoon shade
which lick light off the grass, off the rooftops,
nothing creeps the blue walls. The three pictures
repose in entirely blank absence.

My office disappears before me as
a meadow goes away before deep night.
All that is left is desire with no keys.
His hand finishes dialing. I answer.

ANSWER TO A LOVER

An exultation takes us outside life.
—Theodore Roethke

You say we meet outside our skin.
We sing what stones desire to sing.
Pressing me closer than the day,
You seal my bones with a brief ring,
For you believe your blood's harangue.
You grow exact reluctantly.

Regret, my noisy Love, regret.
For things should stay within their skin
And stones should neither hear nor sing.
We are not one another's kin.
For who can join you bone to bone?
Who are you? What ring is this ring?

I practice what is possible,
Keeping my lonely hands and eyes.
I silence what is loud and hot;
From silence sometimes you arise,
Arise beyond yourself with grace.
What might be comes from what is not.

IN THE RESTAURANT

If I could, I would describe a man
leaning over the sea at midnight
in an olive windbreaker,
the cleats of his boots planted in fists of rock
his veins twisting like lifelines in his hands,
which tow, are towing at a hemp rope.
Hand over hand he pulls it in,
an impossible mess of song he must unravel.
He plays it like a kite
while the humpbacked dark leans close and squints,
while the ocean licks its chops.

Safe in a restaurant with my child,
who is learning how to use a fork,
I see through the curtained window
the moon being hauled backwards, north.
In its glass the water goes loose.
No one, not even the child notices.
While we continue playing word games, I think
so that's what he does at night
and that's why his boots are wet;
so he pulls that long sound out of the moon.
My hands for once go slack to listen.

III.

PAVANE FOR THE DEATH OF A COMPOSER'S SON

He suffered, the neighbors said.
Shoulderblades hollow as a whistle.
There was never any floor beneath his feet,
but only bass notes in odd beats
over which he learned to pick his way.
Through the ceiling he could see summer sky.
Sparrows flew in the windows in fall,
and in fall hectic leaves collected
in the corners of his papa's scherzos.
Public records say that
the only solid structure in the house was the stairs
and that even his father's third quartet
could not keep him in.
One day when the old men arrived,
smelling of rosin and linseed oil,
and unpacked their instruments,
the boy crouched behind the red settee
to listen, his elbow sticking
through the wall into the snow.
When they began tuning up with scales
the little bag of bones began ascending.
On the solid planks of music
he climbed and climbed,
higher than a piccolo,
beyond shrill winter air,
through octaves of the sky.
He could not be recovered.
When they found him that night,
his father shook him and shook him
and dusted the snow from his mute collar
and passed a hand in front of the moon.
On the day they covered the boy with earth
a hundred measures of silence became his tune.

THEIR WEDDING

Not so much that he could not stand
coming home by the railroad crossing under the streetlight
to his beige room with its bed and table
on which he kept a wooden bowl of nuts
and to the papers which by Thursday night sounded
like the dry rattle of the leaves' throats.

Not so much that she could not defy ·
the shrewd appraisal of sightseers
who drove the bad end of State Street in hard sunlight
to find a bargain in the steep streets strewn with
popcorn boxes, stockings, and condoms
on Sunday morning during the hour her mother took communion.

But that a strange wind moved their hands to touch,
A strange priest struck them dumb and married them.
All languages became their native tongue.
They learned to live in one another's places, where all signs
refer to sums not yet computed, where all words
are not yet found and worried into lines.

THE HOLDUP AT SOPHIE'S LUNCH TRUCK

Every morning at seven Sophie's husband backs her lunch truck
through the debris at the dead end of the street,
pulls the brake, shouts goodbye in Greek, and hops the bus for home,
leaving Sophie to drive her truck all morning slowly into the sun.
One morning when it was 92° before nine o'clock
ghosts rose from the coffeebeans earlier than usual
and a host of spinach and feta pies wheeled toward God
like the hubcaps of sixteen saints' appetites perfectly finished.
In spite of the fan put there to keep it down, the truck
had gotten beyond the telephone wires by ten,
when a man cool as a pinstripe stepped in and saw
the doughnuts whooping it up in their glass cage,
the baklava going nuts, the spoons clucking their tongues with joy.
"This is a holdup," he said. "I'll take the silver."
Pulling a gun, he lined his palm with quarters,
his scowl glinting in all George Washington's eyes.
But Sophie, who was frying a cheesesteak to heaven,
driving her truck into the sun, didn't know.
The pinstripe, ascending every second against his will,
cocked the trigger, looked down the barrel at her,
and let her go.

THE BLACKHAIRED CARPENTER

for Morris Collier

Go past the lawns, which are now giving way
to shadow and there he stands again on
the veranda of Mozart's third concerto
in black wingtip shoes, mopping his brow,
turning his handkerchief as if it were a page
of a sacred book to mop again, and hoisting
up a flat note with his frown.
                              He taught us
the severe logic behind sound: position
exact as the degrees of a vase. Hold your
hand like this. No, like this. There. Make your wrist
remember how that feels. The wrist
arches its neck and flutters to remember.
You try too hard, he says. Don't you know the music
will hold you? Trust its eyebeams, its bannisters
turning on themselves.
                              Listen: on the porch
of every concerto stands a short, dark
carpenter, hands dirty with rosin.
He comprehends only the octaves he has made
He swings the heavy hum of the G string
into place and good gravity holds that
until he lays another sound on top of it.
At his feet the sawdust whines and
fidgets like an obedient animal.

But down the steps, across wide lawns
he does not see three chestnut bays
eating up the hillsides, steadily emptying
the world of grass and forget-me-nots,
neighing cadenzas away as they circle
the house, arching their necks like wrists
that cannot remember, and staring
at the blackhaired carpenter with bloodshot eyes.

PERU: AUGUST 12, 1964

It seemed a rainbow at first,
that arc in the lucky dawn,
falling from the highest peak of the Andes
to the *barriadas* in this valley
where women part their black hair,
glance at the sky and hoist into slings
niños who wail "mama."

Raking my heart tonight
to find what I have lost
I find their faces placid and humble
as beds which have been waiting
through years of sunlight and falling shadow
for the comfort of hands
which will never return

for I am remembering again today
how I drove down an old road
full of switchbacks marked with iron crosses
to learn at the bottom
how the sky over the *barriadas* was bisected that morning
by the gallant yellow curve of the bus
in which all their children were falling.

WHAT THE WEST WIND KNOWS

The west wind gales around
the girl sitting on a rock
who watches a dolphin stitching the waves
and thinks of how it would feel
to have that head heavy on her lap,
to be staring into that intelligent eye,
to inhabit a knowledge of bright fish,
to understand the currents' supplication
and the ragged longings of seaweed.

To think of this makes her no less
a girl sitting on a rock
while the gulls above her continue to spin
like pieces of tinfoil in the air
uttering their claptrap sounds
while darkness cast by nothing visible
slides like the shadow of a knife
through the brown water beneath her feet.

Yet she is more than a girl,
not stitching the waves but
thinking of how it would be,
which is itself a thing
pure as what the west wind knows
when it escapes her lungs as song.

ARIADNE

She first caught sight of him
in the courtyard while tossing a golden ball
which she hoarded to dream on later
after Dionysus queened her to his gorgeous night.

In her sixteenth year, during one of
those games, Theseus sauntered into sight:
slave, neat as a summer storm, quick
wrists flicking his leather bonds.
Thyme bloomed where he walked.

He was the evening's entertainment.

He met the bull carelessly,
his hands and feet laughing off the dumb back,
his temperate eyes singing home to their mark until
he buttoned up a somersault too fast.

Where the bull's horn raked him,
drops of blood grew like ripe cranberries,
his pulse beat in her brain
and she staggered under his hurt gaze.
They bore her to her rooms.

In the ring, lucid with pain, he finished the bull.
The audience tore up mountains and hurled them into the sea.
He nodded, his wounds already locking, and slipped out.

He stayed with her until the season
when naked trees stand out like bones
against the salmon flesh of sky.

Often in the dark hubbub of wine
while her older hands cradled the cool ball
she thought of his noons:

How simple he had been with her, how accurate.

SHE BRINGS HIM HOME

And so your husband is safe, and he will
come soon; he is very near, not far away,
and it will not be long before he returns.
    —The Odyssey, Book XIX

Accepting the shawl of light and
the thought of light and the actual
yellow jonquils nailing the patient ground,
she sits by the window,
            casting out her thread and
            drawing in her thoughts,
weaving, weaving.
He has come with a clairvoyant eye,
            not the man himself
            but the old desire for him,
            the prophet,
and cold staggers under a new weight of sunlight.
Time is for her to bear the warmth again
for her mind turns around, turns around and
the trees start pitying with green their own bare sticks,
the clouds start pacing across the unmoved sky,
the violent scent of lilacs starts staining the air.
            Laying aside her thread,
                she straightens her shoulders and
leans into the terrible gaiety of spring.

PROMETHEUS

Pulling the red door shut
behind me one still noon, I knew
that in all streets and waterpipes, in every apricot
lay my ruin, which I had already walked,
drawn from, eaten. The choirs of my mother's blood,
the tiny voices of the earth's pebbles
sang alleluias of desolation on the day
I was conceived. I have never worn any shoes
but those in which to bring fire.
Swatting a gnat, scratching my arm,
everything was the same.

So I walked down the road strewn with stones
named with the names of my old months
back to my beginning. I knew myself
by bringing fire.
                                        And they?
I see their confused eyes clear like
the changing register of orioles' song
each time the eagle does his job.
        By the pitons of an old plot
they have fixed me here. Over and over again
I shut the same red door. At night
they jacket me with ice. All day
I listen for the sincere feet of mice on the rocks.
        Waiting for the eagle's dive my ears grow lucid.
        Listen.
A snail crawls up the black precipice.

PYTHAGORAS UNDERSTANDS HIS THEOREM
AND SACRIFICES TO THE MUSES IN THANKS

On a cliff over the sea
he sits and sets his thoughts
against the drag of moonlight, which is
pumping the tides in and out, which
is spilling young lambs on the hillsides,
which is turning his grandmother, in her grave,
to water.
    Against betrothals and tides
he braces his arms,
against dewy pomegranates he
shuts his teeth, against the
moonlight he tries to commit
the last act of the devout,
to fasten the truth in place
with whatever instrument
can be fashioned.
    His foot rests
on the altar of cold rock
while something hammers his mind
like a sharp question
through the moon
to the light on the other side.
    Beyond the moon
the light rivets him
to its eventual, permanent point.
    Leading his cattle to the rock,
he harangues their necks with a knife
until blood scalds his sandaled feet.

CARTOON FOR SHOSTAKOVICH'S FIRST SYMPHONY

The Conductor's hand flutters,
an osprey in the air and
crashes, beak first,
into an arpeggio.

Two minutes later
we enter the deep chords,
at sea, all of us,
submerged.

The black whale cruises past,
sprouting a spray of staccato notes.
Wise-eyed cellos
dive and roll in his wake.

Deeper and deeper we sink.
The clarinet darts and glints
between us:
little brother mackerel.

We rake bottom,
our hearts scraped knuckles,
private and ravaged
as seaweed in the murky dank.

We are the ruinous sea we batter in.
We resign our reason,
cancel our intellect,
abandon our future appointments.

Up, then, we
clutch to the beam of a tune.
The threshed and disheveled sea
prepares itself to find a shore.

At the edge, the bassoon
frets on stork's legs.
Zook zook zook.
What land is this

where the bearded frown
of a curlew
drops its clams
on the rock of a kettle drum?

Opened, gasping, blankeyed,
we lie awash
on the dark shore
of the stage.

A BESTIARY FOR THE BIRTH OF CHRIST

for E. Daniel Larkin

I. The Frog

Ferns steam and boil beneath the sun.
The cypress tree lets down its hair.
The summer lull waits to begin
till gold has fallen everywhere.

I sit beneath a leaf's dark toe
and listen to the apples swell.
They ripen to what God must know.
They gaze down on the lowly shell.

I do not know what apples mean
nor what perfume the orchid smells,
nor why the bear's eyes flame with sun,
how young lambs foam upon the hills.

But still the garden fills my ear.
the apple nestles in the air
humming its color, bright, gay, dear,
till silence loses poise and then

The light lies on us all like doom.
The gold cracks. Look. And through that gap
time pours its minutes. In a dream
I close my bottom eyelid up.

The swindle snake slips from his hole.
"Malice, Malice," it is done.
With that word, ferns turn into coal
and God becomes a man.

II. The Cow

The wind strolls and licks my bones
with its rough tongue as I lie dimming
in the moonlight on this desert.

All for me is desert now and I all bone:
a thigh whining like a piccolo
on eternal, sound-swallowing sand.

I am the sand's foundering ship.
It barks its glass shins on my skull.
I go down to drowning with my knowledge.

Five years ago, in the season when the locusts
split their skins, I stood lowing in the stall.
I tell you, he was the son of God.

Now time buzzes through my bridge.
There is no heaven for cattle.
My collarbone arches, hollow, hollow.

III. The Raven

I am the most highly developed of birds,
    order Passeras,
    family Corvidae,
    a bird with a wingspan exceeding a yard
    and a well-tailored sense of irony.

I flew over the waters for Noah
and helped Flokki locate Iceland,
but since Poe, I have argued "Nevermore."

From my modern height I have surveyed the frog and the cow.

The frog, natural enemy of the snake, has in his own way
related the myth that says malice snapped the branch
of eternity which crashed end over end,
scattering us off our perch into lurid time.

The cow longs for salvation, believing that such exists.
Not having been present in the stable myself,
how can I authorize the reliability of a witness who was?

I, who can fly, know eternity
when my wings slice it.
Time is the meat in the stubble
between hedgerow and wire fence.
If the most capable of all birds
cannot pick God out of the air,
we must learn to be satisfied with meat.

Only occasionally the wise, frail eyes of the
fieldmouse disturb me and
sometimes I grow
dizzy.

HAYDN'S CREATION:
ARDMORE PRESBYTERIAN CHURCH, 1978

Out of the dark we gather to try to make
the world. Removing scarves, we squint at light.
The bass shakes out the wrinkled hills and I
administer the tune to God tonight

so that he will be able to go on
creating fish and fowl. Damage of bells
and damage of the dawn has worn him out
His voice lies down; his hair grows thin and falls.

The varnish of this floor is worn by paces,
by pressure of prayers and by slow weight of stones.
Here every lucky color drifts to gray.
Here hands that held bright thread relapse to bones.

Yet in the broken edifice of things
where tired angels wear their shawls of dust
contraltos rise again like early sun.
Cellos resolve the morning like a fist

unclenching in the savage presence of
a lover's eyes grown level with desire.
So God, the lover, opens the shut centuries,
shuddering owls and sheep down in fire.

Then all things recognize themselves again.
Giraffes step into bodies, stretch and pause.
Monkeys, hand over hand, learn their own ways.
Field mice balance the moon in tactful paws

till first days break back to the end of time
and man once more in pain puts on his skin.
Astonished knuckles bruise the air again;
snuggle of arteries pumps the wild blood in.

And we break out, rounding a curve of air,
plunging ahead of tempo, O sweet tune.
The light curls through the latticework of stone,
dawns on the angels' wooden cheeks. Is gone.

WHEN THE SEMINAR IS OVER

When the seminar is over
at four o'clock, they fold up Shakespeare,
agreeing to stop thinking
about how Lear's kingdom is his grave.
The students wave and recede
into the small distance,
stocking caps dwindling
to a Medieval illumination.
Finally they disappear.
A typewriter that has been
pecking at its little seeds all afternoon
dozes quietly. Gray douses the walls.
The room grows sullen
under his gaze.
The desk keeps its counsel.
The chair refuses its usual idiom.
No platitude of light remains.

In the corner stand books
which he has picked clean.
Odorless, hair gone,
nails gone, larynx and tongue
and heart all gone,
mute as white bones in a dim cave.

He reads death in them.

The spines wear no flesh,
no meaning, nothing,
not one thing but his ravenous look.

And then no act of living
can save him from the book.

THERE CONVEYS MEANING

The linguist begins his lecture with etymology,
pointing out that silly has pejorated from holy,
that hippopotamus meant river horse in Greek,
that bonfire comes from the fires
barbarians used to build to lick their enemies' bones,
and that empty adverbials such as *very*
lie strewn carelessly around the language now
like the vacated shells of junebugs
on the back sidewalk in summer twilight.

While on the subject of vacancy, he takes up *there*.
You can do anything with *there*, he says.
Take, for example, There was a storm.
There does not just stand in for something else.
There does everything a noun can do.
It can be made passive: There was a storm predicted.
Or it can be made possessive:
There's having been a storm yesterday was surprising.

There is not merely a dummy subject.
There inflects like a noun.
There is substantive.
There conveys meaning.
There will teethe, peel, vibrate, and bruise like a real noun.

There.

And he looks at the girl in the back of the room
In the vacant chair.

ON THE LANGUAGE WHICH WRITES THE LECTURER

This lesson will be on language.
Wittgenstein once asserted that
every language has a structure
concerning which nothing can be said in that language.
We will talk only about what can be said in English.

Our language belongs to the Indo-European group,
subgroup, Germanic. The controllable
units of English are nouns, pronouns,
adjectives, participles, gerunds, verbs
(parsable and unparsable) and dangling modifiers
however inexactly, which convey meaning.

Words are symbolic.
All language is symbolic.
This means that language swallows whole
whatever it refers to and becomes itself the fact.
We will talk only about what can be said in English.

Suppose this: whenever you sit beside a certain girl
you feel a random peace, plain as
cows grazing in the same direction on a hillside.
You think of her and the cows graze in you.
When you evict her, they go.
Therefore she grazes in you often.

Suppose you then say, I have fallen in love.
This is a symbolic statement.
English is an alternative to the language of grazing cows.
Your symbolic English statement neither
slaughters the cows nor brings them home.
You must invent another statement for those facts.

English merely comments on the structure
of another language concerning
which nothing can be said.

This lesson has been on language.

THE STATUE IN SPRING

Let's make this one about a lion. And
it might just as well be flanking the Art
Museum steps, paw holding the world down,
falling asleep on peace treaties, bells, wrecked
cars. What love I have goes to such quiet.
He lies more still than any of us can
imagine being. Like the last voice saying
one last thing, frozen so we can see it:
glory of fur and blind absolute eyes,
dreaming us while grit goes on falling through air.

So suppose one day the stone lion lifts
a paw, the sky films gray, the stores close down.
The last heel's cobbled. The wind stops. At two
o'clock by the Museum fountain a
sandwich sticks in my throat. The lion turns his
head, casually shaking off sunlight,
clearing his mind of the idea of us.
He gets up, kneads the marble and slowly
strolls off like someone we might have loved, now
on his way to becoming something else.